Cake Recipes

TABLE OF CONTENTS

1. CHEQUE WITH RED WINE AND CINNAMON — 6
2. CAKE "LITTLE RED RIDING HOOD" — 8
3. EGYPTIAN CAKE — 10
4. SPIRAL CAKE WITH WHIPPED CREAM AND STRAWBERRIES — 12
5. FINE CAKE WITH APRICOTS AND WINE CREAM — 13
6. CAKE WITH BLUEBERRIES — 14
7. FANCY CAKE WITH BLUEBERRIES, BLACKBERRIES AND PINEAPPLE — 16
8. CAKE WITH YOGURT AND WHIPPED CREAM — 17
9. CAKE WITH APPLES — 18
10. CAKE "LAURA" — 20
11. CAKE WITH MILK — 22
12. PIANO CAKE — 24
13. CHOCOLATE WALNUT CAKE — 26
14. CAKE WITH BERRIES — 28
15. CAKE "SPRING FLOWER" — 29
16. DIPLOMAT CAKE — 30
17. DIPLOMAT FRUIT CAKE — 31
18. FAKE ICE CREAM CAKE — 32
19. OANA CAKE — 34
20. QUICK CAKE WITH CREAM AND FRUIT — 36
21. TOSCA CAKE — 37
22. FANTASY CAKE — 38
23. STRAWBERRY CAKE — 39
24. LEMON MERINGUE PIE — 40
25. FRUIT CAKES "ON VIEW" — 42
26. FRUIT CAKE (STRAWBERRIES) — 44
27. CAKE "SNOWFLAKE" — 45
28. COCONUT CAKE — 46
29. CRUNCHY COOKIES — 47
30. TIGER CAKE — 48

© Copyright 2021 - All rights reserved.

You may not reproduce, duplicate or send the contents of this book without direct written permission from the author. You cannot hereby despite any circumstance blame the publisher or hold him or her to legal responsibility for any reparation, compensations, or monetary forfeiture owing to the information included herein, either in a direct or an indirect way.

Legal Notice: This book has copyright protection. You can use the book for personal purpose. You should not sell, use, alter, distribute, quote, take excerpts or paraphrase in part or whole the material contained in this book without obtaining the permission of the author first.

Disclaimer Notice: You must take note that the information in this document is for casual reading and entertainment purposes only. We have made every attempt to provide accurate, up to date and reliable information. We do not express or imply guarantees of any kind. The persons who read admit that the writer is not occupied in giving legal, financial, medical or other advice. We put this book content by sourcing various places.

Please consult a licensed professional before you try any techniques shown in this book. By going through this document, the book lover comes to an agreement that under no situation is the author accountable for any forfeiture, direct or indirect, which they may incur because of the use of material contained in this document, including, but not limited to, —errors, omissions, or inaccuracies.

31. THE "ELEPHANT EYES" ROLL	49
32. PANDISPAN ROLL WITH PINEAPPLE AND COCONUT	50
33. "TAVALITA" CAKE WITH COCONUT	51
34. CAKE WITH WAFER SHEETS	52
35. CAKE WITH STRAWBERRIES	54
36. CAKE WITH COFFEE AND COCOA	55
37. CAKE AMANDINA	56
38. CARAMEL CAKE	58
39. CAKE WITH APRICOT CREAM	60
40. APRICOT CAKE WITH CHOCOLATE	62

1. CHEQUE WITH RED WINE AND CINNAMON

Ingredients:
- 6 eggs
- 300 grams of sugar
- 200 grams of butter
- 300 grams of flour
- 170 ml of dry red wine
- 1 tablespoon vanilla essence
- 1 teaspoon cinnamon
- 1/2 teaspoon baking powder
- 1 pinch of salt
- garnishes: crushed bitter chocolate, nuts cut into large pieces, candied fruit - whose total weight does not exceed 200 grams
- icing: 5 tablespoons powdered sugar, 1 teaspoon grated cinnamon, 30- 40 ml. of red wine a little butter or margarine and a tablespoon of flour to coat the form

Set the oven to 180 degrees Celsius.

In a bowl, whisk the egg yolks and 150 grams of sugar until creamy, then add the soft butter, in chunks. Beat the butter into the creamed egg yolks. Add flour mixed with 1/2 teaspoon baking powder and additions to taste, add chopped walnuts, crushed chickpeas and candied fruits (pineapple, apricots and raisins), all additions together not exceeding 200 grams. Add the red wine, cinnamon and vanilla essence and mix well. Separately, whisk the egg whites with the salt, add the remaining 150 grams of sugar and continue beating until the sugar is completely dissolved.

The egg yolk, wine and butter mixture is placed on top of the foamed egg whites and mixed very carefully, only with upward movements, with a wide spatula or pear-shaped spatula, so as to lose as little as possible of the air accumulated in the egg whites. In this way, the cake will rise nicely even if it has very little baking powder.

Prepare the tray, greasing it with butter or margarine and then coating it with flour. Pour the cake batter into the prepared pan and level it.

Place the baloney in the preheated oven at 180 degrees Celsius (not ventilated), at a height situated in the middle of the oven. Bake for 45-50 minutes.

After it cools a little, remove the cheese from the cake shape and place it on a grill, on its side, to cool. While it is cooling, turn it a few times from one side to the other.

In the meantime, prepare the glaze, mixing in a bowl the powdered sugar with cinnamon and wine, added a little at a time, until you get a composition of the consistency of a slightly thicker pancake batter. Glaze the warm pancake with this glaze. (You can also glaze with melted chocolate or simply dust with powdered sugar).

After the cheesecake is completely cooled and the glaze is hardened, slice it and enjoy!

2. CAKE "LITTLE RED RIDING HOOD"

Ingredients for the sheet:
- 3 eggs
- 5 tablespoons sugar
- 11 tablespoons flour
- 100 ml oil
- 200 ml milk
- 1 tablespoon honey
- 1 glass of sour cherry brandy
- 2 tablespoons of fresh sour cherries or sour cherry compote, pitted
- 1 teaspoon baking powder

Cream ingredients:
- 400 ml milk
- 1 vanilla pudding
- 1 tablespoon flour
- 5 tablespoons sugar
- 1 tablespoon honey
- 500 grams of sweet cheese
- 250 ml whipping cream
- 1 tablespoon powdered sugar (for whipped cream)
- 1 sachet whipping cream
- 400 grams of fresh sour cherries or a large compote of sour cherries or cherries
- juice from compote (if using fresh fruit, 250-300 ml sour cherry or cherry juice)
- 1 envelope of jelly for the cake

Mix the whole eggs with the sugar, honey and half of the sour cherry brandy, add the milk, oil and flour mixed with baking powder. Mix gently.

Bake the fluid dough in a preheated oven at 175 degrees, in a tray with baking paper, for ten minutes, then sprinkle 2 tablespoons of cherries on top and bake for another 15 minutes.

Leave the baked sheet to cool in the tray, when it is completely cool remove the paper and place on a plate, sprinkling it with the rest of the sour cherry brandy.

Heat 350 ml of milk and honey. Mix the sugar, flour and pudding powder with the rest of the milk and add to the 350 ml. Stir until it comes to a boil and thickens well. Pour the hot pudding over the cheese that has either been strained or blended for a smoother texture, and blend everything together.

Allow to cool completely.

Whip the whipped cream, sweeten and add the sweetener.

Add whipped cream to the pudding and grated cheese mixture, stirring gently. Place all the remaining cherries on the sheet and top with the cream, evenly over the entire surface, smoothing gently with a long-bladed, wet knife.

Prepare the cake jelly according to the instructions on the package, using the required amount of liquid - juice from compote or fruit juice mixed with sour cherry brandy. Cover the cake with the jelly, chill for 2 hours, then cut with a knife dipped in cold water.

3. EGYPTIAN CAKE

Ingredients for one sheet
- 2 egg whites
- 2 tablespoons sugar
- 1/2 tablespoon flour
- 40 g ground hazelnuts

Ingredients for the cream 1:
- 6 yolks
- 6 lbs sugar
- 340 ml milk
- 2 tablespoons flour or starch
- 170 g butter, unsalted
- vanilla essence

Ingredients for cream 2:
- 200 ml whipped cream
- 150 g sugar
- 120 g peanuts, crushed into larger pieces

Start with the creation of the sheets; beat the egg whites until frothy, add the sugar and beat until it melts. Mix the flour with the ground hazelnuts and add to the egg white mixture. Place baking paper on the bottom of a 24 cm baking tin, spread the sheet out nicely and bake over low heat for 25 minutes. In the meantime, wash the utensils and prepare the second sheet. Repeat the action and bake 2 more sheets (in total there will be 3).

After the sheets are made, the cream follows. The 6 remaining yolks from the sheets are mixed in a saucepan with the starch, sugar and gradually added milk. Put the saucepan on the heat and stir constantly until the contents thicken like a pudding, then take the cream off the heat and leave to cool. Stir the butter in a bowl just until "softened" and add a little of the cooled mixture. Add a few drops of vanilla essence and the cream is ready.

For the 2nd cream, melt the sugar and then pour it in a thin layer on a greased pan. Leave to cool and gently peel off, then crumble.

Whip the whipped cream stiff and add the crushed caramel and crushed hazelnuts.

Assemble the cake as follows; place the first sheet, 1/3 of the vanilla cream, 1/3 of the whipped cream. Proceed in the same way with the other sheets. The last layer will be whipped cream.

Refrigerate for a few hours, during which time the caramel will melt a little in the whipped cream. Cut with a sharp knife.

4. SPIRAL CAKE WITH WHIPPED CREAM AND STRAWBERRIES

Ingredients for the sponge cake:
- 4 eggs
- 8 tablespoons of sugar
- 6 tablespoons flour
- 2 tablespoons cocoa
- 1/2 teaspoon baking powder
- 2 tablespoons oil

Cream ingredients:
- 6 eggs
- 150 g sugar
- 1 sachet vanilla sugar
- 250 ml milk
- 20 g jelly
- 500 ml whipped cream
- 250 g strawberries

Ingredients for the garnish:
- 250 g strawberries
- 250 ml whipped cream
- 1 sachet red icing

Beat the egg whites until frothy, then gradually add the sugar and mix until melted. Then add the egg yolks one by one and mix well after each one. Add the oil. Mix the flour with the cocoa and baking powder and then spoon into the egg mixture and mix carefully until incorporated. Pour the batter into a baking tray and bake for 10 minutes in a preheated oven. Remove from the oven on a towel sprinkled with powdered sugar.

Carefully roll and allow to cool.

Prepare the cream while it is cooling; rub the egg yolks with the sugar and vanilla sugar then gradually add the milk.

Place the saucepan over low heat and stir constantly until the mixture thickens slightly. Add jelly dissolved in a little cold water and stir. Leave to cool. When almost cool, pour into a larger bowl and add the whipped cream by tablespoonfuls. Mix well and at the end add the beaten egg whites.

To assemble; cut the roll in 4, roll out the first roll, put 1/4 of the cream then strawberries cut into strips, then some cream and roll.

Do the same with the other 3 and run one after the other.

At the end, coat the cake in the remaining cream and then garnish with whipped cream and strawberries. Pour red jelly over the strawberries.

5. FINE CAKE WITH APRICOTS AND WINE CREAM

Ingredients for the pastry: 250 g French pastry dough

Ingredients for the cream:
- 1 large can of apricots - 850 ml
- 3 sachets of jelly of 7 g each
- 125 ml dry white wine
- 100 gr sugar
- juice of an orange
- 3 yolks
- 400 ml whipped cream

Ingredients for meringue:
- 4 egg whites
- 200 g sugar

Heat the oven to 200 C. Let the dough defrost and roll out. Cut out a circular pastry and place on a baking tray lined with baking paper. Bake for 15-20 min.

Allow the apricots to drain. Soak the jelly in cold water. Heat, stirring, the wine with sugar, juice and yolks. A thick cream will form. Attention! Do not let it boil! Put the jelly on the heat until the grains dissolve and add to the mixture. Stir into the cream until it cools.

When the cream begins to harden, whip the cream. Place a cake ring around the top and spread the top with a third of the cream. Place the apricots on top and add the remaining cream. Refrigerate the cake for 3 hours.

Beat the egg whites with sugar. Cover the cake with the marshmallow mixture, lifting the cake from place to place with a teaspoon. Place the cake in the oven for a short time, leaving it until the tops begin to brown. Garnish with almond flakes.

6. CAKE WITH BLUEBERRIES

Ingredients for the sponge cake:
- 4 eggs
- 4 tablespoons flour
- 4 tablespoons sugar
- 1 tablespoon oil

Ingredients for the cream:
- 1 large yogurt with berries (375ml)
- 500 ml cream for whipped cream
- 20 g jelly
- 3 tablespoons sugar + 2 tablespoons for blueberries
- 150 g blueberries

Ingredients for sprinkling the sponge cake:
- 100 ml hot water
- 1 sachet vanilla sugar

Ingredients for decoration:
- 500 g blueberries
- 1 sachet red jelly

Prepare the sponge cake; beat the egg whites until frothy, then gradually add the sugar and mix well until melted. Gradually add the egg yolks, mixing well after each one. Then stir in the flour a spoonful at a time. Put the mixture into a greased baking tin (diameter 24 cm) and bake for 15 minutes over medium heat. Remove the sponge cake, let it cool, cut it in half and sprinkle it.

Prepare the cream; mix the yogurt with 3 tablespoons of sugar and let it stand for a few minutes. Put the jelly in 3 tablespoons of cold water. Whip the whipped cream (if the whipped cream is sugar-free, add sugar to taste) and let stand for a few minutes. In a saucepan heat 5 tablespoons of water, when it starts to boil turn off the heat and add the jelly dissolved in cold water (leave a spoonful of dissolved jelly, you will need it for the cranberry topping). Stir well and so warm add to the yogurt. Mix well and add the whipped cream mixing well. You get a frothy cream.

Prepare the cranberry topping; put 150 g cranberries in a saucepan, add the 2 tablespoons of sugar, mash a little with a fork and add 3 tablespoons of water. Then put the cranberries on the heat and boil for 5 minutes, add the dissolved jelly and stir well.

Put the first half of the cake in the cake tin, spread and add the cream, leaving 3 tablespoons.

Over the cream, spoon the cranberries with all the juice and stir gently with a wooden whisk. Place the other half of the pastry on top and cover with the remaining cream. Add the 500 g of blueberries.

Put the cake in the freezer. Prepare the jelly according to the instructions on the packet, leave to cool for 1 minute and then spoon over the cake.

Refrigerate the cake for at least 3 hours.

7. FANCY CAKE WITH BLUEBERRIES, BLACKBERRIES AND PINEAPPLE

Ingredients for the sponge cake:
- 4 eggs
- 160g sugar
- 200g flour
- 2 teaspoons baking powder
- 100g grated bitter chocolate

Ingredients for the cream:
- 20 g jelly
- 1 can pineapple (340g)
- 120g sugar
- 250g cottage cheese
- 500ml whipped cream
- 50 ml brown rum (or rum essence)
- 50g chopped bitter chocolate
- 300g blackberries (raspberries, strawberries, sour cherries)

Ingredients for the garnish:
- 200 ml whipped cream
- 250g blackberries
- 2 nectarines
- a few cranberries
- optional 1 sachet transparent jelly

Beat the frothed eggs with 4 tablespoons hot water, sugar and a little salt for about 15 minutes. Incorporate the flour mixed with baking powder and chopped chocolate by tablespoonfuls. Pour the mixture into a greased cake tin (d=26 cm) and bake over low heat for 30 min.

Carefully remove from the cake shape and leave to cool, then cut into 2 layers.

Drain the pineapple from the juice in the compote, then chop finely. Soak the jelly in cold water and separately heat the pineapple juice with sugar. When it is about to boil, turn off the heat and add the jelly. Let it cool a little and add it little by little over the cheese, stirring constantly. Add the chopped pineapple, whipped cream, rum and chocolate.

Divide cream into 3. Place a ring around the bottom pastry, then put 1/3 of the cream, blueberries and 1/3 of the cream, 2nd pastry, remaining cream. Refrigerate for 4 hours and then spread with a layer of whipped cream and garnish with fruit.

8. CAKE WITH YOGURT AND WHIPPED CREAM

Ingredients for the sponge cake:
- 6 eggs
- 250 gr sugar
- 300 gr flour
- 10 tablespoons water
- 1 baking powder

Rub the egg yolks with the sugar, adding a tablespoon of water from time to time, until you get a creamlike syrup. Separately mix the flour with the baking powder and add a little at a time in the yolk mixture. Beat the egg whites until frothy and add to the mixture.

Grease a 26 cm caketin with butter and line with flour, place the mixture in the tin and bake over medium heat for 40 min. Remove to a grill and leave to cool.

Ingredients for the cream:
- 400 g fruit yogurt
- 1 l whipped cream
- 3 tablespoons sugar
- 1 fruit compote of 400 gr
- 20 g jelly (2 sachets of 10 g)

(Try to use similar flavour, for example if the yogurt is peach, use peach compote).

Mix the yogurt with the sugar. Take 3 tablespoons of the juice from the compote and boil it in a saucepan. Separately dissolve jelly in 100 g cold water, then pour over the hot liquid. Do not boil because jelly loses its properties by boiling!

Allow to cool a little and warm mix with the yogurt. Stir in 500 g whipped cream and finely chopped fruit from the compote.

Cut the pastry into 2 or 3 pieces according to preference, sprinkle with the juice from the compote. Put a metal ring around the top and fill with cream.

Leave to cool for 3-4 hours and then garnish with whipped cream and fruit.

9. CAKE WITH APPLES

Ingredients for the sponge cake:
- 4 eggs
- 120 g sugar
- 120 g flour
- 2 tablespoons hot water

Ingredients for stuffing:
- 1,2 kg apples, peeled and cored
- 10 g edible jelly
- 100 g sugar
- 5 tablespoons lemon juice
- 2 sachets vanilla sugar

Ingredients for decoration:
- 470 ml milk
- 1 sachet vanilla pudding powder
- 60 g+40 g sugar
- 1 sachet transparent jelly for cakes
- 1 teaspoon cinnamon
- 1 tablespoon lemon juice
- 250 ml white wine

First prepare the stuffing. Grate the apples (1kg) on a grater with large holes and cook them together with the sugar, lemon juice and vanilla sugar. Add sugar if necessary. When the apples are cooked, turn off the heat, dissolve the jelly in 2-3 tablespoons of cold water and add to the apple mixture. Stir well and leave to cool.

Prepare the pastry; preheat the oven on low heat, rub the egg yolks with hot water and sugar until it melts. Gradually add the foamed egg whites and flour, mixing over the top.

Bake in a greased and floured (or parchment-lined) 24 cm tin for 20 minutes. Allow the pastry to cool and then cut in half.

Make the pudding according to the directions on the packet and leave to cool covered with foil to prevent crusting. Cut the rest of the apples into small pieces and boil for 3-4 minutes with the wine, 40 g sugar, cinnamon and lemon juice. Remove with a slotted spoon.

First the top, then the apple mixture (it should be almost hard when you roll it out, do not be scared it hardens from the jelly),   then the other top, the pudding and the apple pieces. Put in the fridge to chill, cold.

In the meantime, mix the wine remaining after the apple pieces have been removed with the jelly powder and let it bubble for a few minutes. Turn off the heat and spoon the jelly, first in the center and then towards the edges. Refrigerate for 2 hours and then it is ready to serve.

10. CAKE "LAURA"

Ingredients for the sponge cake:
- 6 eggs
- 12 tablespoons sugar
- 11 tablespoons flour
- 1/2 teaspoon baking powder
- 1 tablespoon cocoa
- 3 tablespoons water

Ingredients for the cream:
- 250 ml milk
- 3 tablespoons sugar
- 4 eggs
- 1 tablespoon cornstarch
- 500 ml whipped cream
- 20 g jelly
- 200 g white chocolate
- 50 g milk chocolate

Ingredients for syrup:
- 1 tablespoon sugar
- 2 teaspoons rum essence
- 150 ml water

Ingredients for the garnish
- 500 ml whipped cream
- 1 tablespoon cocoa
- 2 tablespoons warm water

Prepare the pastry; beat the egg whites stiff, add the sugar one by one and mix well until it melts. Then add the egg yolks one by one, mixing after each one. Remove the mixer from the mixer, use the wooden spoon and gradually add the flour mixed with cocoa and baking powder. Bake the pastry in a baking tray lined with baking paper for 15 minutes over medium heat. Remove the pastry to a wooden rack, allow to cool and then cut in half.

Make a syrup from water, sugar and rum essence, boil for a few minutes, then leave to cool. For the cream, first grate the chocolate over a small grater. Mix the egg yolks with the starch and sugar until smooth, then add the milk. Put the saucepan on the heat and stir continuously until it thickens like pudding. When it has reached this point turn off the heat and add the jelly dissolved in 50 ml of cold water. Stir well and then add the grated chocolate. Allow to cool and then stir in the whipped cream. Add the beaten egg whites and the grated milk chocolate.

Spread the pastry and fill with the cream thus obtained. Refrigerate for 1 hour and then decorate.

For the garnish, mix a spoonful of cocoa with 2 tablespoons of hot water and then with whipped cream mixed with a sachet of whipping cream.

11. CAKE WITH MILK

Ingredients for the sponge cake:
- 2 eggs
- 2 tablespoons sugar
- 2 tablespoons flour
- 0,5 teaspoon baking powder
- 1.5 tbsp cocoa powder
- 2 tablespoons warm water

Ingredients for cream:
- 670 ml milk
- 70 g corn starch
- 2.5 tablespoons sugar
- 70 g white chocolate
- 170 g room temperature margarine (or butter)
- 100 g powdered sugar

Ingredients for the glaze:
- 140 g milk chocolate
- 3 tablespoons milk
- 2.5 tablespoons sugar
- 100 g margarine

Blend the eggs with the sugar until it melts. Sift flour, cocoa and baking powder into another bowl and gradually add to egg mixture. Gradually add the water.

Bake in a preheated oven at 180°C for about 15 minutes in a 20 cm diameter tin. You will need to make 2 tops (double the mixture and divide it in two and bake 2 tops or make one bigger and cut it in two).

Mix 100 ml of milk with sugar and cornstarch. Pour the remaining (570 ml) milk into a pot add white chocolate and heat over low heat until it boils. Reduce the heat and add the starch mixture, stirring constantly. Keep stirring until it thickens. You'll know it's thick enough if, when you scrape the bottom of the pot with your spoon, you can see the bottom of the pot. Allow to cool. Mix the margarine with the powdered sugar and add the cream.

Put all the ingredients in a double boiler and heat until creamy. Allow to cool and then blend.

Assembly: 1 sheet of pastry, half the custard, half the icing, then repeat. Cut the 2nd day.

12. PIANO CAKE

Ingredients for sponge cake:
- 5 eggs
- 80 g sugar
- 50 g ground walnuts or hazelnuts
- 24 g cocoa
- 80 g flour
- 8 g baking powder

Ingredients for the roulade:
- 5 eggs
- 100 g sugar
- 1 teaspoon oil
- 2 tablespoons warm water
- 80 g flour
- 8 g baking powder

Ingredients for the cream of roulade:
- 150 g butter
- 100 g bitter chocolate
- 150 g ground walnuts

Ingredients for the custard:
- 40 g starch or 50 g flour
- 150 g sugar,
- 2 sachets vanilla sugar,
- 500 ml milk
- 100 g butter

Ingredients for chocolate frosting:
- 100 g bitter chocolate
- 20 g butter
- 1 tablespoon of water

Blend the whole eggs with the sugar for 10 minutes until frothy, then gradually add the flour, cocoa and baking powder, mixing. Finally add the ground walnut kernels. Bake 2 tops in a 22 cm pan greased with a little fat and lined with flour for 12 minutes at 180 degrees. Remove and leave to cool. You can also make a single pastry cut in two.

Blend the whole eggs with the sugar or 10 minutes until frothy, then gradually add the oil, water and flour mixed with baking powder. Bake in a large (40×32 cm) baking tray at 180 degrees for 15 minutes. Leave to cool.

Melt the chocolate with 100 g of butter on a steam bath or in the microwave. Add the rest of the butter and the ground nuts. Mix well and leave to cool.

Mix the starch with 50 ml of cold milk and add the rest of the milk and sugar. When hot, add the starch mixture and stir quickly. Remove from the heat and leave to cool. When cold, add the butter and mix well.

Place a ring around the first pastry and place over half of the white cream. Cut the roll into 3 cm strips. Spread with chocolate and walnut cream, then roll each strip, placing it on top of the next strip. Roll tightly to form a large spiral and place on top of the pastry. It's easier to grease the rolling sheet, then cut it into strips. Place the other half of the white cream and the other pastry. Refrigerate for 3-4 hours or from evening to morning.

Melt the chocolate together with the butter and water and pour over the cake.

Cut with a knife dipped in hot water.

13. CHOCOLATE WALNUT CAKE

Ingredients for the sponge cake:
- 5 eggs
- 300g of toasted sugar
- 10 tablespoons of water
- 100g ground nuts
- 200g flour
- 1 sachet baking powder

Ingredients for the biscuit:
- 6 egg whites
- 6 tablespoons sugar
- 120g ground nuts
- 1 tablespoon and a half of flour
- a little salt

Ingredients for the cream:
- 6 yolks
- 6 tablespoons sugar
- 350ml milk
- 2 tablespoons cocoa
- 250g margarine
- 2 tablespoons food starch
- rum essence
- 50g grated chocolate

Ingredients for syrup:
- 2 tablespoons sugar
- 1 teaspoon rum essence
- 150 ml water

Ingredients for decoration:
- 500 ml whipped cream

Beat the egg whites stiff, add the sugar and water and beat constantly until a glossy meringue is obtained. Mix the flour with the ground walnuts and baking powder. Gradually add the egg yolks and mix well. Then add a spoonful of the flour mixture and mix over the top with a wooden spoon. Spread the mixture into a larger pan and bake for 15 minutes over medium heat.

Beat the egg whites until frothy, add the sugar, mix well until it melts. Mix the ground walnuts with the flour and add gradually. Bake in a pan lined with baking paper and bake for 20 minutes on low heat.

Mix the egg yolks with the sugar, starch and cocoa, gradually add the milk and put everything on low heat, stirring constantly. It will thicken like a pudding at some point. Take the mixture off the heat and leave to cool. Mix the margarine a little, then add a little of the cooled cream. Finally add a little rum essence and grated chocolate.

For the syrup, boil the water with the sugar and when it boils a few times add the rum essence.

Cut the pastry in half and sprinkle with the sprinkles.

Top with a biscuit top, cream, biscuit top, cream, biscuit top. Finally coat in whipped cream and garnish.

14. CAKE WITH BERRIES

Ingredients for the sponge cake:
- 8 eggs
- 8 tablespoons flour
- 8 tablespoons sugar
- 1 sachet vanilla sugar

Ingredients for the cream:
- 450 gr frozen berries
- 150 gr sugar
- 15 gr jelly
- 500 gr whipped cream
- 100 gr chocolate
- 150 ml berry juice

Beat the egg whites stiff, then add a tablespoon of sugar, beat until the sugar melts, add the yolks in turn, ready with the mixer, move to the wooden spoon, add a tablespoon of flour and mix to get the fluffy pastry. Bake in the oven. Leave to cool and cut in 2.

Thaw the fruit, crush it in the blender together with the sugar. Separately melt the jelly, add to the heated juice, mix well then pour over the berries.

Whip the whipped cream, and add the fruit or rather the fruit puree. Add melted chocolate.

Cut the pastry in two and sprinkle a little (you can use a syrup of 100 ml water, 1 tablespoon sugar, 1 teaspoon vanilla essence), fill with cream and leave to cool for a few hours.

15. CAKE "SPRING FLOWER"

Ingredients for the sponge cake :
- 5 eggs
- 170 gr sugar
- 1 salt powder
- 85 gr flour
- 85 gr starch
- 1 teaspoon baking powder
- 2 tablespoons cocoa
- 50 gr melted butter
- grated zest of 1/2 lime

Ingredients for cream and garnish:
- 10 gr jelly
- 1 sachet vanilla pudding powder
- 500 ml milk
- 3 tablespoons sugar
- 150 gr strawberries (up to 250gr)
- 2 tablespoons peach juice
- 300 gr peaches from compote
- 100 ml whipped cream
- 50 gr grated chocolate

Heat the oven to 200 degrees C. Beat eggs with sugar and salt; add flour mixed with starch, baking powder and cocoa. Carefully fold in the melted butter and lime zest.

Place the mixture in a 24 cm tin lined with baking paper; bake for 10 min. Reduce the heat to 180 degrees C and bake for another 20 min. Remove, leave to cool and cut into 3 pieces.

Soak jelly in cold water. Prepare the pudding according to the instructions on the packet, remove from the heat and add the jelly. Allow to cool. Slice the fruit.

Place a ring of cake around the bottom cake top, sprinkle with juice from the compote and place a layer of cream and then 1/3 of the fruit.

Repeat the operation with the other 2 tops, the last layer being fruit. (On top you can put jelly transparent to make the fruit shine more beautifully).

Leave to cool for 2 hours.

Cover the edge of the cake with a layer of whipped cream and sprinkle with grated chocolate.

16. DIPLOMAT CAKE

Ingredients for the sponge cake:
- 8 eggs
- 8 tablespoons sugar
- 8 tablespoons flour
- 1 tsp baking powder

Ingredients for the cream:
- 6 eggs
- 6 tablespoons sugar
- 250 ml milk
- 30 gr jelly
- 500 ml whipped cream
- 100 gr raisins soaked in rum
- 350 g pineapple chunks

Ingredients for the garnish:
- 500 ml whipped cream
- 2 sachets hardener
- raw fruit or fruit compote: tangerines, peaches, kiwi.
- 1 sachet transparent jelly dissolved according to the instructions on the sachet

Beat the egg whites until frothy, add the sugar one at a time and beat until melted, add the egg yolks one by one and mix well with the mixer then leave it out and mix with a wooden spoon.

Add flour and baking powder a little at a time and mix slowly. Pour the pastry into a greased and floured 26 cm diameter tin and bake in a preheated oven for 20 minutes on medium heat. Remove the pastry, leave to cool and cut in half.

Rub the egg yolks with the sugar, add the milk a little at a time and boil over a bain-marie, stirring continuously until it thickens like thin cream. Dissolve the jelly in 100 ml of cold water and add to the hot cream. Leave to cool.

When it begins to thicken, mix in whipped cream, whipped egg whites, raisins and pineapple. The result is a fluffy and delicious cream.

Put a ring of cake around the bottom top, sprinkle with a little juice from the compote, put the cream on then the top top also sprinkled and chill for 5-6 hours or overnight.

Whip the whipped cream with the whipping cream and spread with a spatula on the cake. Garnish to taste with fruit and pour warm jelly over.

17. DIPLOMAT FRUIT CAKE

Ingredients for the sponge cake:
- 8 eggs
- 15 tablespoons sugar
- 16 tablespoons flour
- 8 tablespoons cold water
- 2 sachets vanilla sugar
- 1 teaspoon baking powder

Ingredients for the cream:
- 6 eggs
- 6 tablespoons sugar
- 1 l whipped cream
- 250 g fruit from compote
- 300 ml milk
- 30 g jelly

Beat the egg whites until stiff, add the sugar gradually alternating with water and beat until a glossy meringue is obtained. Add the egg yolks one by one, stirring constantly, then remove the mixer and gradually add the flour mixed with baking powder, stirring with a wooden spoon. Bake the cake for 25 minutes over medium heat.

Rub the egg yolks with sugar, add the milk and then put them on the steam bath stirring constantly until they thicken like thin cream. Add the jelly dissolved in a little compote juice.

Separately cut the fruit into cubes, beat the whipped cream and egg whites. When the milk and egg mixture is almost cold, add the whipped cream, whipped egg whites and diced fruit.

Cut the pastry in 3 and sprinkle with juice from the compote, fill with cream and chill overnight.

18. FAKE ICE CREAM CAKE

Ingredients for the sponge cake:
- 6 eggs
- 12 tablespoons of toasted sugar
- 1 teaspoon baking soda
- 10 tablespoons flour
- 2 tablespoons cocoa
- 2 sachets vanilla sugar

Cream liners:
- 4 egg yolks
- 2 tablespoons flour
- 200 ml cold milk
- 200 g butter
- 100 g powdered sugar

Icing ingredients:
- 4 egg whites
- 200 g sugar
- 2 sachets vanilla sugar

Beat the egg whites until stiff, add the sugar one at a time and beat until a glossy meringue is obtained. Then add the egg yolks one by one, remove the mixer and mix with a wooden spoon, add the bicarbonate mixed with a little flour, flour, cocoa. Bake the mixture in a baking pan lined with baking paper for 25 minutes on medium heat. Remove the top and leave to cool.

Rub the egg yolks with the flour, gradually add the cold milk and cook over a steam bath, stirring constantly until thickened. Allow to cool, stirring occasionally. Cream the butter and sugar together and gradually add to the cream mixture, stirring constantly.

Steam well until thickened and hardened and then beat until cool. Cover the cake with the cream, then put the icing and shave the chocolate. Chill for a few hours and then cut.

19. OANA CAKE

Ingredients for sheets:
- 200 g flour
- 50 g lard (or 100 g butter)
- 100g powdered sugar
- 1 teaspoon ammonia
- 1 egg
- 1 tablespoon cocoa
- 2 tablespoons milk

Ingredients for the sponge cake:
- 6 egg whites
- 170g sugar
- 1 vanilla sugar
- 100g flour
- 150g cut up shit
- 150g toasted and ground walnuts

Cream ingredients:
- 6 yolks
- 150 g sugar
- 1 tablespoon water
- 250 g butter
- 2 sachets vanilla sugar

Icing ingredients
- 150 g household chocolate
- 50 g butter
- optionally chopped nuts or pistachios

For the sheets, mix all the ingredients and make 2 sheets that are baked on the bottom of the pan over medium heat. Cook very quickly for about 3-4 minutes. When they turn brown around the edges they are ready. Use an ordinary baking tray.

For the batter, beat the egg whites well, then gradually add the sugar and mix until it melts. Add the flour a spoonful at a time, stirring, then do the same with the walnuts and finally add the grated grapes (cut with a knife through the flour).

Bake the pastry in a pan lined with baking paper for 15 minutes on low heat. When done, remove and let cool.

For the cream; rub the egg yolks with the sugar and a tablespoon of water on a steam bath until thickened. When cool, gradually add the butter and vanilla sugar. Mix well.

Put sheet, cream, top, cream, sheet and then chocolate frosting (melt chocolate together with butter over low heat or steam bath).

Sprinkle chopped nuts.

Leave to stand in the fridge overnight and cut with a knife that is kept slightly in hot water (so that the glaze does not crack when cutting).

20. QUICK CAKE WITH CREAM AND FRUIT

Ingredients for the sponge cake:
- 8 eggs
- 8 tablespoons flour
- 8 tablespoons sugar
- 1 sachet vanilla sugar

Cream ingredients:
- 1 cake topper or pandispan
- 2 sachets vanilla cream
- 750 ml milk
- 1 pineapple compote
- 3-4 kiwi
- 1 sachet jelly

Beat the egg whites stiff, then add a tablespoon of sugar, beat until the sugar melts, add the yolks in turn, ready with the mixer, move to the wooden spoon, add a tablespoon of flour and mix to get the fluffy pastry. Bake in the oven. Leave to cool.

Drizzle the compote syrup over the top. Prepare the cream according to the instructions on the envelope then spoon over the top. Put the fruit cut into pieces and pour over the jelly prepared with the remaining juice from the compote.

Put the cake in the fridge (it hardens very quickly) and then cut with a knife dipped in cold water.

21. TOSCA CAKE

Ingredients:
- 8 eggs
- 200g sugar for the cake and another 8 tablespoons for the cream
- 50g coconut
- 100g mac
- 4 tablespoons flour
- 1 sachet vanilla pudding powder
- 300g margarine or butter
- 250g chocolate
- Cocoa biscuits probably 300g - to cover the tray in which the cake is made
- 300ml milk
- 1 baking powder

The batter is made from 8 whites beaten to a froth and 200g of sugar is gradually added. Then add 50 g coconut + 100 g poppy and finally 4 tablespoons of flour + a baking powder quenched in lemon juice. Pour the mixture into a greased and lined pan. Bake in a preheated oven for 15-20 min.

Cream: 8 egg yolks + 8 tablespoons sugar rub well. Add 300 ml milk and 1 sachet of vanilla pudding. Boil the mixture in a bain-marie until it thickens like mayonnaise. When cold gradually add 300 g margarine or butter, mixing well. Spread the cream evenly over the pastry.

On top of the cream, place cocoa biscuits next to each other. Pour melted chocolate over the biscuits.

Refrigerate overnight and cut with a slightly heated knife.

22. FANTASY CAKE

Ingredients:
- 5 eggs
- 200 g sugar + 50 g
- 200 g flour
- 10 tablespoons water
- 1 sachet baking powder
- 2 sachets vanilla sugar
- lemon peel
- sour jam (preferably plum)
- 150 g ground nuts

Rub the egg yolks with the sugar, add a little by little water until you get a cream like syrup. Dissolve the baking powder with the lemon juice, and gradually add it together with the flour. Bake the pastry over medium heat for 30-40 minutes.

When it is baked let it cool then spread with jam, add ground walnuts then whites beaten foam with 50 g sugar.

Place in the oven over high heat until the meringue on top browns a little.

Allow the cake to cool and cut with a knife dipped in water.

23. STRAWBERRY CAKE

Ingredients:
- 4 eggs
- 1 cup sugar
- 1 cup yogurt
- 1 teaspoon baking powder
- 1 cup flour
- 1 packet vanilla sugar
- 250g fresh strawberries
- 3 tablespoons sugar
- 100 ml water

Mix the eggs with the sugar until the sugar melts and the mixture increases in volume. Add the yogurt and flour mixed with baking powder. Finally add the vanilla sugar.

Bake in a tray lined with baking paper for 15 minutes at 180 degrees, then leave to cool.

Separately blend the strawberries then mix them with sugar and water. Let it simmer for a few minutes and then drain the seeds. Leave the syrup to cool and then with a fork prick the top and pour the syrup over.

Cut the puddle in two and place one piece on top of the other. Just sprinkle the top and top with whipped cream.

24. LEMON MERINGUE PIE

Ingredients for the crust:
- 260g flour
- 1/2 teaspoon salt
- 110g cold butter
- 60 ml very cold water

Ingredients for the cream:
- 200g sugar
- grated rind of one large lemon (14g rind)
- 60g food starch
- a pinch of salt
- 320 ml cold water
- 70 ml strained lemon juice
- 4 egg yolks

Ingredients for meringue:
- 4 egg whites
- 8 tablespoons of sugar

First crust is made. Put flour and butter cut into pieces in a bowl. Rub with a fork until the mixture becomes sandy. Add a spoonful of very cold water and mix. When the dough has come together, roll into a ball, cover with foil and chill for 30 minutes.

Preheat the oven to 160 degrees C.

Roll out the dough, spread it on a baking sheet, then lay the tray for orientation, about as large as the dough should be rolled out. The dough should extend 2 cm beyond the edge of the tray. Turn the tray over, then peel off the baking sheet and arrange the dough neatly. Cut the extra. Prick from place to place with a fork.

Place the sheet back over the dough and put beans in the middle to prevent the dough from rising when baking. Bake for 10 minutes, then remove the sheet and bake for another 5 minutes to brown nicely all over.

Leave to cool and prepare the cream. Wash the lemon well with hot water then wipe and shave it. There should be 14g of grated peel. Put the sugar, starch and lemon zest in a saucepan. Mix well and add the egg yolks. Stir, add lemon juice and water. Put the saucepan on low heat, stirring continuously and when it starts to thicken, keep the cream on the heat for exactly 1 minute, then turn off the heat and let it cool a little.

Prepare the marshmallow. In a dry bowl, whisk the whites froth with a little lemon juice. Add the sugar a little at a time and beat until all is melted. Into the baked crust, pour the lemon cream, level off nicely and then add the meringue. Touch the back of the spoon to the marshmallow and pull it up to give it a moist shape.

Bake in the oven over low heat for about 10 minutes, until the meringue is light brown. Remove to a grill to cool. Serve after refrigerating for at least 2 hours.

25. FRUIT CAKES "ON VIEW"

Ingredients for 24 pieces:
- 200 ml milk
- 25g fresh yeast
- 1 egg
- 2 tablespoons oil
- 1 tablespoon butter
- 500g flour
- 2 tablespoons sugar
- 1 sachet vanilla sugar
- 1 tsp salt
- grated lemon and orange peel

Ingredients for filling:
- fruit
- little sugar

Ingredients for greasing:
- 1 egg yolk
- 2 tablespoons milk

Ingredients for syrup:
- 4 tablespoons sugar
- 6 tablespoons water

Heat the milk a little and put the yeast in it. Let it stand until it loosens and liquefies. In a smaller bowl mix the egg with the sugar, vanilla sugar, salt, add the melted butter and oil. Sift the flour into a larger bowl, add the egg mixture and milk with the yeast. Knead well until the dough is elastic and comes away from the bowl. Allow to rise covered for an hour.

If using fruit from the compote, cut pieces and let them drain in a sieve. Roll the dough out on a floured board, knead a little and divide into 24 pieces. Press each piece lightly with your fingertips to form a circle. In the middle put some pieces of fruit, a little sugar, then pinch the ends together gently.

Place in a tray lined with baking paper, leaving a little distance between them as they will rise when baked and leave to rise for 15 minutes.

Preheat the oven to 200 degrees. Brush the cookies with the beaten egg yolk and bake until lightly browned (7-10 minutes). In the meantime prepare the syrup. Bring the water and sugar to the boil and boil for 3 minutes. Remove the cakes from the oven and spread with hot syrup.

Allow to cool a little and then eat them.

26. FRUIT CAKE (STRAWBERRIES)

Ingredients:
- 4 eggs
- 150 g sugar
- 150 ml milk
- 8 tablespoons oil
- 1 sachet vanilla sugar
- 400 g flour
- 1 sachet baking powder
- grated zest of 1/2 lemon

Optional:
- 2 egg whites
- 100 g sugar

Mix the eggs well with the sugar and vanilla sugar until the vanilla sugar melts. The result will be a frothy cream. Add the oil and mix for 3 minutes.

Gradually add flour mixed with baking powder, alternating with milk and stir until incorporated. You can use the mixer on low speed, no need for a wooden spoon. At the end add the grated lemon zest.

Pour the mixture into a large pan and place the chopped fruit on top. Bake for 15 minutes over low heat.

Top with the 2 egg whites beaten with the sugar. Bake for 2-3 minutes until the meringue is browned.

Allow to cool and cut the cake into pieces with a knife dipped in water. If no meringue is used on top, dust with sugar.

27. CAKE "SNOWFLAKE"

Ingredients for the sponge cake:
- 5 yolks
- 180g sugar
- 1 sachet vanilla sugar
- 200g flour
- 8g baking powder
- 10 tablespoons water

Ingredients for the cream:
- 250g margarine
- 350ml milk
- 100g coconut
- 1 tablespoon food starch
- a little rum essence

Ingredients for the glaze:
- 5 egg whites
- 200g sugar
- coconut or white chocolate

Mix well the egg yolks with the sugar, vanilla sugar and the 10 tablespoons of water until the sugar melts and the mixture doubles in volume. Add the flour mixed with the baking powder and mix gently. Bake in a baking sheet lined pan over medium heat for 15 minutes.

For the cream, mix the coconut with the starch, add a little milk and then put the mixture on low heat. Allow to cool and add a little essence. Rub the margarine a little in a bowl to loosen it, then add a little of the coconut mixture and mix well.

For the glaze, whisk the egg whites with the sugar on a steam bath until the mixture becomes slightly stiff, then leave to cool.

Place the cake, then the cream, then the icing and top with coconut or grated white chocolate.

28. COCONUT CAKE

Ingredients for sheets:
- 500 gr flour
- 150 gr sugar
- 100 gr margarine
- 1 baking powder
- 1 teaspoon cocoa
- 1 egg
- 70 ml milk

Mix well, divide in 2 and make 2 sheets.

Coconut cream ingredients:
- 6 egg whites
- 200 gr sugar
- 200 g coconut
- 150 ml milk

Whisk the egg whites until frothy, gradually add the sugar until a glossy mousse is obtained, like meringue. Brush the coconut with hot milk and then leave to cool. Add to the egg whites.

Place the first sheet in a greased and floured pan, then the coconut mixture, the 2nd sheet, prick with a fork and bake over medium heat for 40 min. Remove and leave to cool.

Cream ingredients:
- 6 yolks
- 6 tablespoons flour
- 250 gr sugar
- 300 ml milk
- 1 packet butter (200 gr)

Mix the egg yolks with the flour and sugar, pour in the milk gradually and then place on the steambath stirring continuously until thickened like cream. Allow to cool and mix with the rubbed butter. Spread over the cake and top with grated chocolate.

29. CRUNCHY COOKIES

Ingredients for crispy cookies:
- 120g oat flakes
- 150g butter
- 1 tablespoon sugar and 1 sachet vanilla sugar
- 4 tablespoons pear nectar
- 3 eggs
- 150g flour
- 150g coconut flakes
- 1 teaspoon baking powder
- 100g chocolate
- 4 tablespoons candied cherries, chopped finely
- 4 lbs oat flakes
- 4 tablespoons corn flakes
- 4 tablespoons almond flakes
- 2 tablespoons honey

Fry the oat lakes until golden brown (without oil!). Mix the butter with the egg and nectar (compote juice). Then gradually add flour mixed with baking powder, coconut flakes and cooled oat flakes.

Wrap the dough in plastic wrap and refrigerate for an hour. Heat the oven to 180 degrees. Form the dough by hand into discs and place them on a greased baking tray lined with baking paper and bake for 15-17 min (they should be golden brown).

Remove and leave to cool. When cool, cover with a mixture of candied cherries, oatmeal, cornmeal and almond flakes all mixed with honey. Decorate with melted chocolate.

30. TIGER CAKE

Ingredients:
- 250 g butter (margarine)
- 250 gr sugar
- 2 sachets vanilla sugar
- a pinch of salt
- 4 eggs
- 250 gr flour
- 50 gr starch
- 1/2 sachet baking powder
- 75 ml milk
- 2 tablespoons cocoa

In a bowl put the melted butter with the sugar, vanilla sugar and a pinch of salt, mix well then add the eggs one at a time. Mix the flour with the starch and baking powder, add to the dough, alternating with 50 ml of milk. Divide the dough in two, and in one of the halves put cocoa, the remaining milk and mix well. Grease a pan with butter and line with flour.

The dough is placed like this: Place a spoonful of the yellow dough in the center, then top with a spoonful of cocoa dough and repeat. Do not spread with a spoon as the dough will set by itself.

Bake for 1 hour until done.

31. THE "ELEPHANT EYES" ROLL

Ingredients for the sponge cake:
- 6 yolks
- 8 egg whites
- 10 tablespoons sugar + another 32 tablespoons water
- 1 baking powder (15g)
- 5 tablespoons flour
- 10 g ground nuts
- grated lemon and orange peel

Ingredients for the cream:
- 150 g nuts, toasted and then ground
- 2 sachets vanilla sugar
- 5 tablespoons of milk
- 250 g butter
- 2 tablespoons powdered sugar
- We need 2-3 more bananas

Optional whipped cream for decoration or melted chocolate

Mix the egg yolks with the sugar and water until the sugar has melted and the mixture has doubled in volume. Add grated lemon and orange zest. Beat the egg whites until stiff and then gradually add 3 tablespoons of sugar. Place the beaten egg whites on top of the egg yolk mixture, mix with a wooden paddle and gradually add flour and ground walnuts.

Bake the pastry in a large pan on the stove (lined with baking paper) for 8-10 min on low heat. Leave to cool slightly and then turn out onto a wooden board.

For the cream mix the ground walnuts with sachets of vanilla sugar and powdered sugar and thicken with 5 tablespoons of hot milk. Put it in the fridge and then add in the cold butter a little at a time, mixing well. Add a few splashes of rum essence.

Spread the cream on the pastry, then cut the pastry in half and put peeled bananas on each half and sprinkle a little lemon juice to prevent oxidation.

Roll up tightly (no fear, don't break the top) and refrigerate the rolls.

Top with finetti, whipped cream or melted chocolate.

32. PANDISPAN ROLL WITH PINEAPPLE AND COCONUT

Dough ingredients:
- 4 eggs
- 100 gr sugar
- 1 sachet vanilla sugar
- 100 gr flour
- 25 gr starch
- 60 g coconut flakes

Ingredients for cream and garnish
- 1 can pineapple rounds (340 g)
- 400 ml whipped cream
- 1 sachet whipping cream
- 100 g coconut flakes, candied cherries

The oven is heated to 180 degrees C. Line a baking tray with baking paper. Beat the egg yolks with 4 tablespoons of cold water, the icing sugar and the vanilla sugar. Beat the egg whites and add 1/3 of the quantity to the egg mixture. Add flour mixed with starch and 1/2 the amount of coconut flakes. Add the remaining egg white and fold in. Spread the mixture in the pan, bake for 10 min.

Remove and place on a kitchen towel sprinkled with coconut flakes. Peel off the baking paper and roll the pandispan in the towel.

To prepare the filling, let the pineapple drain and cut into pieces. Whip the whipped cream with the sweetener. Leave some whipped cream aside for decoration, and incorporate 50 g of coconut flakes and pineapple cubes in the rest.

Spread the sheet with coconut filling, roll, and chill for 60 min.

Then dust with the remaining coconut flakes. Sprinkle with whipped cream. Garnish with pineapple chunks, candied cherries and coconut flakes.

33. "TAVALITA" CAKE WITH COCONUT

Ingredients for the sponge cake:
- 350 g sugar
- 70 g margarine
- 2 eggs
- 2 tablespoons honey
- 200 ml milk
- 1 baking powder
- 400 g flour

Ingredients for the glaze:
- 200 g powdered sugar
- 200 g butter or margarine
- 100 ml milk
- 100 g rum or rum essence(10 ml)
- 2 tablespoons cocoa
- 200 gr coconuts

For the pastry, mix all the ingredients together and place in a greased and floured baking tray. Bake over low heat for 25-30 minutes. When cooled cut into cubes.

Set the cubes aside and prepare the glaze; boil all the ingredients until they boil. Take the pot off the heat, roll the cubes in the glaze and then cut in the coconut.

Place on a platter and refrigerate.

34. CAKE WITH WAFER SHEETS

Ingredients:
- 1 packet of wafers
- 350g plain biscuits (crushed in food processor)
- 250g soft butter
- 100g sour cherry brandy
- 30g rum essence (or 1 vial of essence)
- 200ml milk
- 200g ground walnuts
- 300g sugar
- 100g cocoa
- 1 sachet chocolate icing

Mix the sugar with the cocoa and milk, which is put in a saucepan to boil until the sugar is completely melted. Remove from the heat, add the sour cherry brandy, rum essence and butter.

Separately in a bowl, mix the nut crackers, add over the hot syrup and mix everything very well.

Spread the wafer sheets with this cream and top with chocolate frosting (according to the instructions on the envelope).

Cut and serve, after cooling.

35. CAKE WITH STRAWBERRIES

Ingredients for the sponge cake:
- 100 g bitter chocolate
- 150 g chocolate biscuits
- 12 candied cherries
- 100 g chopped almonds
- 100 g butter

Ingredients for cream and garnish:
- 1 sachet vanilla pudding powder
- 1 tablespoon starch
- 500 ml milk
- 70 g sugar
- 200 ml whipped cream
- 10 g jelly
- 4 tablespoons orange liqueur
- 200 g cottage cheese
- 700 g strawberries
- 50 g chocolate
- 3 tablespoons almond flakes

Melt the chocolate for the top in the microwave or if you want to use a vintage bain-marie method. Crush the biscuits and chop the candied cherries. Mix everything with the chopped almonds and melted butter. Place in a cake tin lined with baking paper, press by hand to even out and refrigerate for about an hour.

Clean the strawberries, put the 10 best pieces aside for garnish. Cut the rest into cubes.

Mix the pudding powder with starch and a few tablespoons of milk. Boil the rest of the milk with the sugar and cream. Stir in the pudding mixture until thickened. Allow to cool. Soak jelly in water and microwave to dissolve. Stir the jelly, cottage cheese, orange liqueur and diced strawberries into the pudding mixture.

Spread the cream on the pastry and refrigerate to harden for about 3-4 hours.

For the decoration melt the chocolate and dip the strawberries in it and then put them aside in the fridge for a while to harden the chocolate. Place on the cake and sprinkle with almond flakes. Sprinkle almond flakes on the edge of the cake.

36. CAKE WITH COFFEE AND COCOA

Ingredients:
- 8 eggs
- 2 packets 80% fat butter
- 300g sugar
- 2 tablespoons flour
- 70g cocoa
- 400 ml whipped cream
- 1 bottle of coffee essence

Add 300g sugar + 10 tablespoons water, dissolve over heat, add 70g cocoa and give it 2-3 boils then let it cool. Rub in the foamed butter, add 8 egg yolks one at a time and rub continuously, add the coffee essence. Mix well the two compositions.

A quarter of the resulting mixture is mixed with 8 beaten egg whites and 2 tablespoons of flour.

Bake a sponge cake in a tray lined with baking paper. When you take the pastry out of the oven it is puffed up and nice and fluffy, but not having as much flour as other pastries, it will deflate. Don't panic, this is normal for a cake with so little flour.

When the pastry cools, put the rest of the cream on top.

Refrigerate for 3-4 hours, then coat the cake with whipped cream.

37. CAKE AMANDINA

Ingredients for the sponge cake
- 6 eggs
- 200 g sugar
- 30 ml water
- 30 ml oil
- 20 g cocoa
- 8 tablespoons flour

Beat the egg whites until frothy, add the sugar, mixing until stiff. Then add the water, and the egg yolks rubbed with the oil, and mix with a spoon, from the bottom up, until the egg whites are incorporated. Then add a little of the flour mixed with the cocoa, mixing the mixture. Pour the dough into a not very large pan, greased with oil and lined with flour, and put baking paper on the bottom.

Bake for 30-35 min at 175 degrees, in the last 5 minutes raise oven temperature to 190 degrees.

Leave the pastry to cool, then cut in half.

Ingredients for syrup
- 400 ml water
- 200 g sugar
- 2 chocolate cappuccino sachets

Put all the ingredients for the syrup in a saucepan to boil, and from the moment it starts to boil, leave it on the heat for 5 minutes. Allow the syrup to cool.

Ingredients for the cream
- 3 egg yolks
- 150 g powdered sugar
- 250 g butter
- 3 tablespoons cocoa

In a bowl put the partially melted butter and mix well for 1-2 minutes. Add the powdered sugar and mix until the sugar dissolves. Then add the egg yolks and cocoa and continue to mix for about 1 minute.

Place the first half of the pastry on the plate and sprinkle it, put the cream on top, level it well and then put the other half on top and sprinkle it again.

Leave the assembled cake in the refrigerator for 2-3 hours.

Ingredients for the glaze
- 200 g chocolate
- 150 g liquid cream for whipped cream
- 50 g butter

Put the liquid cream on the fire to heat (careful, without boiling!), then add the chocolate and butter.

Take the saucepan off the heat and stir until the mixture is smooth. The icing remains soft and creamy even after it hardens.

Stir in occasionally until cool, then pour over cake, slowly, starting from the center.

After frosting the entire cake, refrigerate for at least 1 hour.

38. CARAMEL CAKE

Ingredients for the sponge cake:
- 5 eggs
- 200 g powdered sugar
- 4 tablespoons cold water
- 100 g flour
- 2 sachets caramel pudding powder
- one sachet baking powder

Ingredients for the cream:
- 10 tablespoons of sugar
- 200 ml milk
- 250 ml whipped cream
- 3 eggs
- 1 tablespoon food starch or flour
- 10 g jelly

Ingredients for the glaze:
- 6 tablespoons brown sugar
- 6 tablespoons liquid whipped cream
- 100 g butter

Ingredients for syrup:
- 1 tablespoon sugar
- 100 ml water

Whisk the egg whites with the powdered sugar and cold water. Add the egg yolks one at a time, mixing with a paddle. Then add the flour mixed with the pudding sachets and baking powder and mix well. Place the mixture in a greased and floured pan. Bake in a heated oven for 30-35 min at medium heat. After it has cooled, cut the pastry in thirds.

Melt the sugar over low heat until caramelized, then add the hot milk, stirring quickly. Separately rub the egg yolks with the starch, add the hot syrup and put on the heat stirring constantly until it thickens like cream. Add the jelly dissolved in a little cold water. Allow the cream to cool and then stir in the whipped cream and whipped egg whites.

Place one side of the cake on a plate and drizzle with a little syrup (melt the caramel sugar and pour 100 ml of water over it and let it boil until all the sugar melts). Place the ring of the cake tin around the top and put 1/2 the cream. Repeat with the other parts of the cake. Refrigerate for 2-3 hours.

Caramelize the sugar, while caramelizing heat the liquid whipped cream thoroughly with the butter.

Pour hot cream and butter over the sugar, mixing well until all the caramel sugar is melted. Cool the icing in cold water and when it begins to thicken pour over the cake.

39. CAKE WITH APRICOT CREAM

Ingredients for the sponge cake:
- 6 eggs
- 200 g sugar
- 30 ml water
- 30 ml oil
- 20 g cocoa
- 8 tablespoons flour

Ingredients for apricot cream:
- 250 g apricots from compote
- 1 small yogurt with apricots
- 250 ml whipped cream
- 50 g powdered sugar
- 7 g jelly

Ingredients for the glaze:
- 200 g chocolate
- 150 g liquid cream for whipped cream
- 50 g butter

Beat the egg whites until frothy, add the sugar, mixing until stiff. Then add the water, and the egg yolks rubbed with the oil, and mix with a spoon, from the bottom up, until the egg whites are incorporated. Then add a little of the flour mixed with the cocoa, mixing the mixture. Pour the dough into a not very large pan, greased with oil and lined with flour, and put baking paper on the bottom.

Bake for 30-35 min at 175 degrees, in the last 5 minutes raise oven temperature to 190 degrees. Leave the pastry to cool, then cut into three pieces.

Puree the apricots in a blender or with a stick blender, then mix with the powdered sugar until it melts.

Hydrate the jelly in a little compote and heat gently over the heat, stirring until dissolved. Stir in the whipped cream and yogurt. Put the ring of the cake tray around the first sheet of cake, put the cream on top, then again cake-cream-cake. Refrigerate for at least -3 hours.

Put the liquid cream on the heat to warm, then add the broken chocolate cubes and butter. Take the saucepan off the heat and stir until the mixture is smooth. Stir in occasionally until cool, then pour over the cake, slowly starting from the center.

Refrigerate for another 1-2 hours and then garnish.

40. APRICOT CAKE WITH CHOCOLATE

Ingredients for the sponge cake:
- 6 eggs
- 200 g sugar
- 30 ml water
- 30 ml oil
- 20 g cocoa
- 8 tablespoons flour

Ingredients for apricot cream:
- 250 g apricots from compote
- 1 small yogurt with apricots
- 250 ml whipped cream
- 50 g powdered sugar
- 7 g jelly

Ingredients for the glaze:
- 200 g chocolate
- 150 g liquid cream for whipped cream
- 50 g butter

Beat the egg whites until frothy, add the sugar, mixing until stiff. Then add the water, and the egg yolks rubbed with the oil, and mix with a spoon, from the bottom up, until the egg whites are incorporated. Then add a little of the flour mixed with the cocoa, mixing the mixture.

Pour the dough into a not very large pan, greased with oil and lined with flour, and put baking paper on the bottom.

Bake for 30-35 min at 175 degrees, in the last 5 minutes raise oven temperature to 190 degrees. After baking let cool and cut into thirds.

Puree the apricots in a blender or with a stick blender, then mix with the powdered sugar until it melts.

Hydrate the jelly in a little compote and heat gently over the heat, stirring until dissolved.

Mix everything with whipped cream and yogurt.

Place the ring of the cake tray around the first sheet of cake, put the cream on top, then again cake-cream-cake.

Refrigerate for at least -3 hours.

Put the liquid cream on the heat to warm, then add the broken chocolate cubes and butter.

Take the saucepan off the heat and stir until the mixture is smooth.

Stir in occasionally until cool, then pour over cake, slowly starting from the center.

Refrigerate for another 1-2 hours and then garnish.

www.ingramcontent.com/pod-product-compliance
Lightning Source LLC
Chambersburg PA
CBHW062201100526
44589CB00014B/1908